This book belongs to:

____

Made in the USA
Middletown, DE
24 November 2019

79319183R00066